ACQUIHIRE TRANSACTIONS IN INDIA: ITS SCOPE AND PERSPECTIVE

VOLUME 2, ISSUE 1 OF BRILLOPEDIA

ROHAN ANIRAJ | VIVEK MALHOTRA AND RITWIK RAI

ISBN 979-888591829-9

Contents

Preface

"Start writing, no matter what. The water does not flow until the faucet is turned on".

-Louis L'Amour

Hundreds of students and professors are contributing their work to Brillopedia, we are here to provide ample information about Law and Contemporary issues. Our aim is to provide a platform for today's generation to express their views and ideas on law and contemporary law.

Publication

This research paper is published in volume 2, issue 1 of Brillopedia

Authors

Rohan Aniraj

Vivek Malhotra

Ritwik Rai

CHAPTER ONE

Abstract

With the arrival of synthetic intelligence, the Internet of things, huge records and the cloud, attracting top-degree engines have has come to be one of the maximum essential elements to compete in one's profitable rising sectors. Top tech companies, along with Google, Facebook, or Cisco has currently begun out obtaining startups, now no longer vital for his or her product or service, however for his or her talents. This phenomenon is called "acquihire", which is a mixed painting of "acquisition" and "hire". In this Research paintings, we appearance ahead to speak about the purchase system is pretty just like an ordinary M&A.

From traders' perspective, they may receive a commission lower back nearly the same (plus actual inflation rate) quantity they invested. Hence, an ordinary M&A is tons higher for VCs, due to the fact they acquire capital gains. As for acquiree's personnel, they're given an extremely good amount of money with "golden cuffs", shares that vest over a 3-6 period, so they're relatively stimulated to live with inside the organisation and the duration of "golden cuffs" is decided with the aid of using the mission there are assigned to. This monetary incentive shape is nicely designed to hold the acquiree's personnel within side the organisation. Some of the troubles related to M&A is cultural differences, however, in this acquihire case, it does now no longer come to be a problem, due to the fact acquiree isn't compelled to conform to the acquirer's tradition. For example, in case you are received with the aid of using Alphabet, you don't always need to be Googlers, which reduces the danger of M&A.

Keywords:-Acquihire, Mergers and Acquisitions, Statrtups, Market Growth , High Financial Gains.

CHAPTER TWO

INTRODUCTION

Acquihiring is a broad concept with the combined neutralization of two major concepts- hiring and acquisition. The concept deal with authenticating the procedure to acquire companies and to hire employees and staff for the same. Acquihiring or talent acquisition is considered the finest way to buy out a companies' working resources or the employees considering their skill set and expertise in particular fields that would benefit the acquiring company at large. The established orthodox companies are quite rigid and not flexible in conveying this approach. Therefore, the startups are everyone's first choice as they are flexible, extremely focused, hardworking, and easy to acquire considering their size and presence in the market. It is considered a cosmetic gain as it benefits each and every one. The investors get desired returns, employees benefit through bonuses and the parent company achieves their set goals.

The concepts of Acquihire focus more on acquiring the skills and talents of the workforce, rather than the services the startup offers as a company. Whereas an acquisition is equally devoted to acquiring both the workforce and the business conducted by them. "An Acquire has two commonly used structures." In the primary structure, the parent company buys up the assets of the startup and hires its workforce. Investors are benefited from this structure as they gain back their investment, whereas the founder suffers loss by not gaining any equity from acquiring the startup. The secondary structure is very similar to that of a normal recruitment procedure where the company employs the workforce of the startup and remunerates them a modest ransom before the company's dissolution. [1]

The government's Make in India initiative is cultivated to support the manufacturing masses of the country to rise and expand in the global market, while simultaneously luring foreign countries to consider India as the best option to invest their resources and outsource information. The government's policies also safeguard vulnerable Indian companies from takeover by foreign giants. The process of acquihiring not only provides financial supports to small startups facing a shortage of funds but also helps traditional companies realize their data and analytical aspirations. Seeking the new outlook of data innovation in the western countries, USA most importantly have jumped up the pace of numerous budding companies. When it comes to a developing country like India, it has also shown a slow yet significant growth in business visionary companies and with every passing day is pacing up to make up the lost time. Indian Companies like redbus.in, Make my Trip, Naukri.com, Ola, Flipkart, Zomato, etc., tends to cover the market hole for squeezing needs of the mass. These startups aim to meet the wants of the masses and therefore are putting utmost efforts to fulfil the wants of a heterogeneous population of a billion minds. The companies practice in different fields and demand different skillsets like medical care, transportation, food, instruction, IoT, and so on. India's startup economy has gained pace with time. Demands are being supplied and outsourced, and consideration has expanded over several continents. The advent of Digital India Campaign has given a big boost for the coming up of new companies and its market growth, not only in India but multi nationals.

In recent past there has been a significant change in the societal outlook of large companies. The time calls for a surge shift from capitalism to innovation. The base of this shift is dependent upon careful investment in human resource. The modern standard for corporate responsibility would mean accountability in the era of digitalization. Therefore, the era calls for investing in human resources over technological assets. The innovative approach to inputs, outputs and performance are key aspects in shaping the acquisition and merger policy of tech giants. Through various research and approaches it has been deducted that "the absolute size of the knowledge bases is directly related to the post acquisition innovation output." This method is considered as a key step for product development where supply is limited as compared to the demand. It would result in resolving key innovation problems, by acquiring skilled workforce[2].

[1] 1 Jessica Dabiri, How Does an Acquihire Work?,PillsburyPropel (May 18, 2020, 10:30 AM),

<https://www.pillsburypropel.com/guidance/how-acquihire-work-startup>

[2]   'Acqui-Hiring',   Collar   Search   (Aug   13,2020), <https://www.collarsearch.com/blog/acqui-hiring-a-game changer-at-the-time-of-covid-19/>

CHAPTER THREE

ACQUIHIRE AND THE EMERGING TREND IN TALENT ECOSYSTEM

The time for growth is now. We have seen a sharp increase in acquihire from year 2017. This could be attributed to the startup boom which happened in years 2014 and 2015 which is now seeing those startup deadpool due to inability to scale, unable to beat competition or not being able to find a product market fit. Technology companies and successful starups are quick to grab on to this opportunity and are absorbing these teams. In year 2018'19, 27% of all acquihire were made by Indian MNCs, 35% were made by global MNCs and a staggering 40% by successful Indian startups.

Companies benefit a great amount when they acquihire startups. The first clear benefit is of building technological capabilities. With the rapidly changing technology landscape, it is very important for tech teams to be able to up-skill their talents. When startup brings to the table talents which is already up-skilled, already tried and tested, it is of great value to them. The second benefit is that of market expansion.[1] We have observed that 93% of acquired startups operated in the same industry as their acquirer. With big companies trying to build platforms or their products, startup team which have niche talent in a particular industry could bring great relevance to building used cases for particular features. Case in point of a leading Indian travel Platform. What they did was they had a great online platform for their customers. They acquihired a team which provided last mile connectivity and an offline experience thereby creating value add on the customer's end on both online and offline channels. The third is an added benefit. It is that of an Entrepreneurial culture. As company grow larger in size their propensity to take risk reduces drastically. By absorbing entrepreneurs into their teams, they are able to keep up with highly focused, resulted oriented work. They bring to the table various methodologies which startups use to scale and that could be very important for companies which are looking to compete with their competitors[2].

"Some of the top Acquihire transactions from India are as follows":

1. **Intel-Ineda System:** 100 engineers from Ineda Systems core team were acquihired by intel for an exclusively undisclosed amount in February 2019. The acquihire was purely based to absorb the skillset of the engineers in low power SoCs and graphics for enterprise and consumer application.
2. **Airtel Acquihiring Quikmile and AuthMeID Services:** To boost the innovation factor in the area of AI, AR, VR, and IoT; Airtel acquihired AuthMeID, a Bangalore based AI solution startup and Quickmile, a Gurugram based tech enabled logistic startup.
3. **Vokal - StupidChat:** StupidChat a quizzing app firm was acquihired by the Bangalore based news and awareness sharing platform in an exclusive confidential deal in May 2019. The six-member team of StupidChat founded in Kolkata was engaged in daily awareness product for the Vokal platform.
4. **Lendingkart – KountMoney:** Lendingkart a no deposit taking non-banking financial company(NBFC) acquihired Kountmoney a lending app for private loan in july 2016. It helped the company to fulfil the data analytics and technological capabilities and further boost the general purpose of the startup.
5. **Apple – Tuplejump:** The seven-member team of tuplejump who worked as analysis and data mining platform was acquihired by Apple in April 2016. The employees along with the founder now work at different offices at Apple.[3]

While acquihire seem like a great benefit to the acquirer they also pose certain risks. The first is that of how the deal is structured. The acquirer needs to be very careful in understanding how the deal is structured especially when it comes to paying out the investors and sponsor of the startup. The second risk comes from the post-closing liabilities. To prevent this the corporate should always engage a legal team to ensure that their directors do not face any liabilities or conflict of interest when it comes to absorbing or acquihiring a startup. The third and the most important risk is that of change management. We often see that when acquihired startup gets observed into a company, the team faces a culture shock. It is extremely imperative for the acquirer to ensure that his team internally changes its culture to foster entrepreneurs. With acquihire increasing sharply in India, it is very evident that the benefits outweigh the costs. With startup culture slowly integrating itself into larger companies in India, it is a great sign that India is maturing in terms of technology and innovation.

[1] Ashna Ambre, 'Acqui-hiring: Trending now in India', Livemint, (Aug 15, 2020, 2:45 p.m.),

<https://www.livemint.com/Companies/PmI220a2SVdicqEGjYBeEM/Acquihiring-Trending-now.

[2]https://www.cooleygo.com/acqui-hire-basics/

[3]https://whatis.techtarget.com/definition/acqui-hire-talent-acquisition

CHAPTER FOUR

PROCESS OF START-UP AND ACQUIRE IN INDIA

<u>Start up in India</u>

"In recent years, initiatives have begun to gain more attention in many parts of the world. In India, the number of startups has increased rapidly and more support is now available at all levels. Due to the great potential of early trade, India is often described as the child of the emerging market poster.

Today Startups are widely recognized as important engines for growth and productivity. By innovating and uncontrollable technologies, initiatives can produce influential solutions, and thus serve as vehicles for socio-economic development and transformation.

However, there are still many challenges that serve as a barrier to realizing the true power of initiation in India."

<u>OPPORTUNITIES AVAILABLE</u>

India now has 38,756 officially recognized startups - with 27 unicorns, eight of which have acquired the status by 2020 - and is the third largest technology implementation center in the world. Apart from that, the Indian economy, demographics and effective government support provide a wide range of start-ups that are effective.

India's Economic Growth: Just before the sudden disruption of the Covid-19 epidemic, India's economy continued to grow and purchasing power was slowly growing. With short-term economic recovery expected, rising spending will be driven by modest wage growth and high-income segments.

Therefore, the size of the Indian market offers ample opportunity for beginners to grow. Popular demographics: Indian populations are another benefit. Half the world's population is under 25 years old. About 700 million people born in the late 1980's to the 2000's are materialistic and have the power to waste.This makes them a large part of the people who have the ability to absorb the inventions and services provided by the startups.

Active Government Support: The Government of India launches the flagship program, "Startup India" in 2016. The plan aims to build a strong ecosystem that helps the growth of start-ups and initiates business transformation.

In addition, the restructuring of the digital payment ecosystem is led by State Innovation (NPCI), through Aadhaar, Jan Dhan, UPI, and India Stack.As India improves its digital connectivity, barriers to market access have been eased and created the first positive ecosystem.High Range in Rural Areas: With the majority of Indians still living in rural areas, many initiatives focus on providing easy living in rural areas. [1]

For example: FIA Global - with a network of 26,000 banking agents - uses Artificial Intelligence (AI) to deliver financial products and services such as remittance and credit services in rural areas, and has reached more than 34 million customers. MFine provides a powerful AI healthcare platform for people to contact more than 3,500 doctors.PharmEasy connects local pharmacy stores and diagnostic centers to confirm doctor's instructions and deliver more than 100,000 medicines."

<u>**RELATED CHALLENGES**</u>

Challenges From Regional Inequality: India is a very diverse country with a wide range of cultures, languages, races and religions.

As a result, beginners' understanding of them is often limited to certain regions. In that sense, comparative benefits are linked to specific regions. Digital Divide: With about 70% of Indians living in rural areas, customers in the main market tend to come from low-income domains in the valleys. This often discourages many beginners from coming up with a pan-India approach. Funding Problems: To get started, a large amount of operating costs are required. Many startups, especially in the early stages, start with bootstrap, that is, either support themselves by saving the founders' money, or using money from friends and family. Employment Challenge: For many job seekers, joining a startup as an employee is not an attractive career option, given the natural risk of starting out may fail.In addition, many job applicants do not have enough skills. Beginners see a gap between the knowledge that students receive in college and the knowledge needed for careers, especially in areas where technology is rapidly changing.

Complex Regulatory Environment: The Government of India has introduced policies aimed at easing the business environment to get started. However, the current regulatory framework in which startups operate is widely regarded as complex, inefficient and unpredictable.

For example, the government has introduced the "Angel Tax", introduced in 2012 to curb money laundering, but it also does not encourage early investment."

GO FORWARD

Integration with the School Curriculum: National Education Policy, 2020 aims to develop student entrepreneurs by providing vocational education in partnership with industry and introducing coding to school children. This could have a positive impact on India's first environmental program, if business skills are integrated into the education curriculum under the new education policy.

Closing the Digital Diversity: There is a need to close infrastructure spaces esp in rural areas, to promote digital literacy and to help people become more aware of the digital world. In this regard, the government's Digital Saksharta Abhiyaan program is a step in the right direction.

Agri-Startups Development: With the majority of Indian workers still employed in agriculture, there is a need to remove roadblocks and promote agricultural implementation.[1] The new farm regulations give farmers greater choice and encourage newcomers to transform their value chain into finance, finance, transportation, integration and marketing. Startups in High-end Technology: The recently released Draft Space Policy states that "Indian organizations can facilitate the design, development and fulfillment of satellites and related communications systems.They can set up satellite programs."

[1]https://www.upcounsel.com/acquihire

[1]https://www.upcounsel.com/acquihire

CHAPTER FIVE

FOLLOWING ARE THE TOP 10 ACQUISITIONS THAT HAPPENED IN INDIA

1. **FLIPKART-WALMART:** Walmart acquis 77% of Flipkart for $16 billion, it makes it the largest acquisitor involving an Indian company, in the year 2018.
2. **TATA STEEL- CORUS:** In the year 2007, Tata Steel has taken over European steel major Corus for the price of $12.02 billion, which made the Indian company world's 5th largest producer.
3. **VODAFONE- HUTCHISON ESSAR:** Again, in the year 2007, the world's largest telecom company in terms of revenue, then Vodafone made an entered the Indian telecom market by acquiring 52% stake in Hutchison Essar Ltd. Vodafone purchasing 52% stake in Hutchisson Essar for about $10 billion.
4. **HINDALCO- NOVELIS:** Hindalco Industries Ltd. is a subsidiary company of the Aditya Birla Group and Novelis is a world leader in the production of flat-rolled aluminium products. The Hindalco Company acquired the Canadian company Novelis for $6 billion, making the combination entity the world's largest producer in rolled-aluminium.
5. **RANBAXY-DAIICHI SANKYO:** In 2008, Daiichi Sankyo Co. Ltd., signed an agreement to acquire the entire shareholders of Ranbaxy Laboratories Ltd, India. Ranbaxy's sale to Japan's Daiichi was priced at $4.5 billion.
6. **ONGC-IMPERIAL ENERGY:** In early 2009, Oil and Natural Gas Corp. Ltd (ONGC) took control of Imperial Energy, a UK Based firm operating in Russia for the price of $1.9 billion.

7. **MAHINDRA & MAHINDRA-SCHONEWEISS:** In 2007, Mahindra & Mahindra acquired 90 percent of Schoneweiss, a leading company in the forging sector in Germany. This consolidated Mahindra's position in the global market.
8. **STERLITE-ASARCO:** In the year 2009, Sterlite Industries, a part of the Vedanta Group, signed an agreement to acquire the copper mining company Asarco for the price of $2.6 billion.
9. **TATA MOTORS-JAGUAR LAND ROVER:** Tata Motors' acquisition of luxury car maker Jaguar Land Rover was for the price of $2.3 billion, in 2008.
10. **SUZLON-REPOWER:** Wind Energy premier Suzlon Energy acquired RePower for $1.7 billion. Suzlon Energy Limited is a wind turbine supplier based in Pune, India and RePower systems SE (now Senvion SE) is a German wind turbine company founded in 2001, owned by Centerbridge Partners[1]."

[1] https://www.cooleygo.com/acqui-hire-basics/

CHAPTER SIX

HOW ACQUIHIRING IS A GAME CHANGER?

Acqui-hiring by and large happens when a specific range of abilities is highly sought after, for example, network protection and distributed computing. It is named on the parent organizations' prerequisites and holds either an upper hand for them or offers workers that line up with the organizations' objectives. Items and administrations presented by the organizations are regularly stopped by the acquirers and their representatives are alloted to different offices as per the parent organization's necessities. New businesses are more disposed towards getting gained by industry goliaths inferable from their capable pool of representatives, particularly the personalities behind conceptualization and innovation. Numerous new businesses neglect to remain above water monetarily and acqui-hiring goes to their guide.

Acqui-recruits are really superficial in nature as the representatives get rewards, financial backers get a huge return and the parent organization gets the ideal ability to do their capacities. This procedure was initially framed in light of the fact that tech monsters had limitations against recruiting each other's workers as a feature of No-Poach Agreements. In any case, the nature of ability accessible in new companies is unprecedented and is wanted profoundly by enormous partnerships. These people are perceived to be driven, adaptable, calculative, and very engaged, which are the superb characteristics needed in any representative.

What Are the Advantages of an Acqui-Hire?

The number of people qualified to work in the industry is small. Companies with lots of cash flow try to lure top talent. When they can't do that, the acqui-hiring is a great strategy. The number of workers entering the innovation business isn't expanding consequently. With such countless huge partnerships lacking qualified labourers, they want to recruit gifted groups whenever the situation allows. It's a simple way of filling the interest for tech representatives.

A business adds a team of highly skilled professionals who can build apps, create online services, and keep up existing software and hardware. Since the employees already have a strong working relationship, they can start a job with the new company as if they had worked there for years. He spelled it Acquhiring and defined it as a large company buying a small company whose only employees are founders.

How Does the Acqui-Hire Purchase Work for Employees?

In most obtaining, the staff of the bought association will meet for another position. It's identical to some other utilizing in such way. The leaders manage the potential delegates like they are commonplace up-and-comers. Without a doubt, even the coordinators should meet, ordinarily for thing director occupations. Like other new representative screenings, certain people presumably will not advance pleasantly. Any person who bombs the forthcoming worker meeting won't join the new association. An acqui-enroll doesn't guarantee that everyone tracks down another profession. In most obtaining, the staff of the bought association will meet for another position. It's identical to some other utilizing in such way. The leaders manage the potential delegates like they are commonplace up-and-comers. Without a doubt, even the coordinators should meet, ordinarily for thing director occupations. Like other new representative screenings, certain people presumably will not advance pleasantly. Any personwho bombs the forthcoming worker meeting won't join the new association. An acqui-enroll doesn't guarantee that everyone tracks down another profession.

In most acquiring, the staff of the bought association will meet for another new position. It's identical to some other utilizing in such way. The chiefs manage the potential delegates like they are normal up-and-comers. To be sure, even the coordinators should meet, ordinarily for things executive occupations. Like other new representative screenings, certain people presumably will not advance pleasantly. Any person who bombs the imminent worker meeting won't join the new association. An acqui-enroll doesn't guarantee that everyone tracks down another profession.

Acqui-hiring in COVID-19

As seen from past financial emergencies, acqui-recruits increment altogether during and post an emergency. A comparable flood is normal in

2020 as the world's economy lay injured in the wake of COVID-19. The pandemic has essentially expanded digitization prompting a tremendous hole among request and supply of tech work. This has prompted different associations hoping to obtain gifted people in the field of network safety and distributed computing. Numerous associations are viewing at this as a chance to acqui-recruit a security firm or startup to improve their general security.

The current situation is trying for new companies as the market is desolated and there are less freedoms, however acqui-employing could be the most ideal system for them to make due in this downturn. Coronavirus has made different Catch 22s as far as what can be the fate of new companies. In a period where organizations are effectively realigning their labor force to more readily suit the "close to ordinary", acqui-employing can come in very convenient. Associations hoping to procure need to zero in on different variables to guarantee viable outcomes.

Many firms have tracked down an elective which might settle reckless cycles. Perhaps you've heard the expression "Acquihire" (or acqui-enlist). It's a basic blend of the words "procurement" and "recruit." And It implies basically that. Rather than searching for a recently recruited representative or two, you secure a specialty shop practice, a sole expert who accompanies a set up book of business, or significantly another office. The thing that matters is immense.

Rather than tracking down another representative you trust will demonstrate to have the stuff (without any shields) or building another group with new abilities without any preparation, an acquihire can be a fantastic procedure for optimizing the development of your firm. The head or directors of the bolt-on firm is/are demonstrated rainmakers since they have exhibited they can sell.

A startup or an established firm? Book of business and talent?

The type of acquihire you seek depends on your needs. Here are just three of the many types of scenarios you might encounter.

1. Great tech skills, not great business acumen:

Startups (and even established firms) are often founded by bright people with tremendousengineering, design, or development skills. Some eventually discover that theirunderstanding of technology is the easy part of their enterprise. Running the actual business of it is a whole other ball game. Org charts can be messy, and sales may be flat or worse. You may find them to be looking for guidance, for mentors. They may be relieved to fold their substantial skills and vision into the processes and systems that larger, more established firms can provide them. It makes for a great marriage if you pick up an entrepreneurial team with readymade skills and relationships in an area you need, and they can enjoy the benefits of a bigger, more experienced company. It may be a discount deal waiting to be had. It beats your having to create new capabilities from scratch, provides stability for them, and offers a growth path for all. providing each party a real deal.

2. Rainmaker, yes. Admin...not so much.

We all know firms started and run by a natural-born salesperson. Proven rainmakers, these enthusiastic entrepreneurs are skilled in their field of endeavor They have proven they can repeatedly identify and qualify prospects, turn them into clients, and see transactions through to a healthy sale. But they are not so strong in administration and logistics and perhaps have not built much of a structured organization as a foundation for growth. Maybe living, with years of client relationships waiting to be expanded upon or simply added to your roster. They just need to plug into an organization that will let them do what they do best: repeatedly find more clients, sell to them, and hand off the details. Maybe they stay for a reasonable transition time or the long haul. Depending on what you and they need, that can be a win-win that is worth the hunt. And there are lots of creative, very cost-effective, ways to make it happen.

CHAPTER SEVEN

DUE DILIGENCE

Whenever possibilities are distinguished, dive deep into your investigation of the chance. Concentrate all parts of the organization, and invest genuine energy confirming the precision of data you are given. Examine their plan of action, contracts with customers, concurrences with workers and merchants, and whatever other elements that can assist with foreseeing future execution. Search for barricades or arrangement executioners that you can reveal before you go excessively far into the cycle—like overabundance obligation, low staff usage rates, a high proportion of low or non-billable workers, over-adjusting of customers, messy monetary controls, or long rents (perceiving that a portion of these variables can be & with appropriate administration). You should be certain you comprehend the merchant inspiration for selling.

Chemistry: Great science between the merchant's and purchaser's supervisory crews and workers can be considerably more critical to the achievement of the exchange than monetary potential.

Take as much time as necessary to get to know the vital participants. Consider chipping away at projects together before you settle the arrangement. Meeting their key workers. Disclose to them your vision, approaches, methodology, and assumptions. Get some information about their way of life. Do you have similar general mentalities toward strategic scheduling?

Typical deal structures: Small acquisitions and acquihires can usually be accomplished without a high percentage of the cash upfront concerning the overall consideration. The elements of typical offers for acquihire candidates may include:

- The seller retains their assets and assumes their liabilities

- Limited amount of cash at closing (usually $50,000 to $150,000 depending uponthe size of the block of business)
- Employment agreements
- Commissions on the legacy business that transfers
- Commissions for new business generated
- Possibly shares/units in a phantom stock plan or long-term incentive plan

Related to commissions on legacy business, we typically recommend between 8% and 10% of the Adjusted Gross Income (total revenuc minus media and outside services purchased) for the life of the client. For new business generated post-closing, we typically recommend between 5% and 8% of Adjusted Gross Income for 12 to 18 months per client.

CHAPTER EIGHT

RELATIONSHIP BETWEEN CORPORATE GOVERNANCE AND ACQUIHIRE

The relationship among shareholders and administrators and the reliance they have on one another packed with clashing interests and goals which crop up because of these ownership, authority and control. This has additionally been distinguished as a fundamental strategy in various organizations. People who are in production cannot understand each and everything about marketing, people who are in design cannot understand each and everything about finance. The board has an obligation to rehearse great administration, which incorporates attempting to build up a solid corporate culture. While that sounds great in principle, dynamic ways of thinking and thoughts like culture can be difficult to characterize and surprisingly more hard to incorporate. Past that, there's likewise the issue of how to screen and quantify corporate culture. Organizations that are attempting to improve or shape culture need pioneers who can use existing cycles and utilize a purposeful methodology when deciding. Culture begins at the top and the best trial of culture is when things turn out badly. How the board and senior heads handle emergencies and seasons of coercion is consistently a genuine impression of corporate culture. Board conversations ought to incorporate how they can keep a positive corporate culture through troublesome occasions.

In a start ups corporate governance practices and prerequisites need to naturally progress and develop just the way startups advances and develops their productive ambit. The corporate governance requirements develop with the expansion of a startups, being affected by the size of the organization, yet additionally by assumptions for different partners. A startup's corporate administration practices and prerequisites need to naturally advance and develop as the startup advances and develops. The hidden reason is that at each phase of its development cycle, a beginning up has diverse business necessities, distinctive arrangement of partners, and changing legitimate compliances, that require varying corporate administration norms. The corporate administration necessities advance with the development of a startups, being affected by the size of the organization, yet additionally by assumptions for different partners. Now and again the development is only the result of the organization's development and at times the movement is the result of a painstakingly customized plan. We investigate what a beginning up could consider zeroing in on in standing of corporate administration at different phases of its development cycle. Most new companies have an extreme, dubious, and turbulent outset. With more deadly concerns like forthcoming solicitations, faltering customers, and enduring income issues to manage, it very well might be untimely for your beginning up to zero in broadly on corporate administration. At this stage, it could be sufficient to receive a 'check the case' approach and simply meet all compulsory lawful, monetary and bookkeeping necessities. You can benefit of the administrations of outside experts who can handhold the beginning up in compliances. You are then on the correct side of law and can dedicate your time and endeavours to the development of your business.

CHAPTER NINE

ACQUIHIRE AND MERGERS & AQUISITIONS

In the traditional mergers and acquisitions (M&A) space, the using price was the goal of enterprise's products, services, brand, highbrow property, customer base, marketplace percentage, plant, equipment or equipment.

Now, withinside the Fourth Industrial Revolution and the generation of technology, the using price of M&A has shifted. A new awareness of M&A Talent is now an important thing asset for lots of groups, mainly the ones withinside the tech industry. As such, we see a new fashion of acquisitions wherein the personnel of the goal enterprise now shape the using price of the M&A.

This has stimulated the term "acqui-hiring", that's made of the words "acquiring" and "hiring" combined. This new acquisition approach acts as a powerful and the green approach of recruiting a massive organization of talent. It overcomes the postpone as a result of having to scout for man or woman candidates, persuade everyone to sign up for the enterprise and negotiate the phrases for every new employee. One of the first-rate acqui-hires is a goal enterprise which already has a pre-assembled absolutely practical crew prepared to hit the floor walking that the customer can deploy to run unique initiatives as a crew.

Southeast Asia

In Southeast Asia places, acqui-hires are additionally growing. In September 2017, McKinsey & Company, the worldwide control consulting firm, acquired-employed VLT Labs, a virtual product engineering and layout start up primarily based totally in Malaysia, for its crew of designers, builders and product managers. five In 2018, Maxis acqui-employed Optima to enlarge its e-trade crew.

We additionally see Southeast Asian groups looking past the place for acqui-hires. In 2016, Go-Jek, the transportation and logistics enterprise primarily based totally in Indonesia, To enable the setup of The legal professional has to additionally warn the customer to consider whether or not giving a key control position in preference to a percentage switch can be extra commercially or operationally practical. The different options are partial acquisitions

Final takeaways can be The approaches wherein this new acquisition approach will affect the structuring of the deal will retain to change. The fashion of the purchase approach may even retain to develop. As those retain to evolve, so have transactional attorneys.

<u>Conclusion</u>

Typically, the goal company's personnelget hold ofthe bulk of the acquisition money, at the same time asquite a fewshares are traded. The acqui-employedcompanyhave to accept, integrate, and manipulate the ambiguity. As a result, each acquihiring groups and marketershave to be aware about the legal guidelines and documentation concerned in an acquihire deal structure.